Don't Sell Grain to a Bird on Credit

And More Arab Proverbs

Compiled by Stephen J. McGrane

Llumina Press

ISBN: 978-1-62550-453-1--PB
978-1-60594-889-8--EB

Contents

Preface

After my first book of Arab proverbs, *'Trust in God but Tie Your Camel' and Other Arab Proverbs*, was published, I soon started to receive more proverbs from old and new friends all over the U.S.A., and around the world. Once the number exceeded several hundred, I decided I should publish another volume that would be of interest to Western readers.

It has been estimated that there are over seven thousand Arab proverbs. Proverbs play an integral role in Arab life and are frequently used in literature and conversation. As in other cultures, they are a reflection of culture and are used to pass on beliefs and values from one generation to the next.

The proverbs I selected for this volume reflect the wit and wisdom of the Arab people. Since human wisdom is universal, many Arab proverbs also exist in other cultures in various forms with the same or similar meaning. The many Arab proverbs with Western equivalents are a reflection of shared values. For some Arab proverbs in this book, I have included the Western equivalent in quotes following the Arab version. If the meaning of an Arab proverb is not obvious, I have also included a brief explanation.

This collection contains more proverbs and more topics than the first volume, as well as more proverbs that are unique to the Bedouin people. I hope it will provide the reader with more humorous and wise insights into the beliefs and culture of the Arab people. As the Arabs say, "Proverbs are knowledge of the street."

Chapter 1

Age and Experience

The old give the most flavor.

"The blacker the berry, the sweeter the juice."

Shows value and respect for older people and things.

A person begins life as a child and ends life as a child.

If you don't have an old person in your house, go and buy yourself one.

Old people are thought to bring blessings to a home.

Regret not an age on the wane
That leaves behind a new one
Of a good name with good deeds
Throughout life you have won.

A person with an empty heart won't age.

An empty heart means you are carefree and have a clear conscience.

Your age is on your face.

Gray hair is a torch of wisdom.

Death sends its message in gray hair.

Gray hair causes no shame, but shame causes gray hair.

Chapter 2
Anger

Anger begins with folly and ends in repentance.

If you want to see how big a man is, see what makes him angry.

A pious person's anger doesn't last longer than putting their turban right again.

Beware of the calm person's anger and the attack of a tame beast.

Chapter 3

Business

The trader of water will never lose.

The shoemaker is barefoot and the weaver is naked.

"The cobbler's son has no shoes."

Much movement can make much profit.

"Keep the pot boiling."

Don't sell grain to a bird on credit.

Count the rotten ones before the sound ones.

Calculate your loss before your profit.

He sold wheat and delivered barley.

This proverb describes a person who does not deliver what he promised.

Buy as if you were to sell.

Look as I look.

A vendor would say this to a buyer to release him of responsibility for any faulty goods, as if to say "buyer beware."

In business, there is no friendship.

The shop is yours.

A shopkeeper's greeting to a customer.

Sell with a smile and buy with a frown.

If tastes were alike, goods would age in shops.

"Good, cheap, and of good origin" is a bargain that never was.

The good monkey is for fifty and the small monkey is for fifty.

It is up to the customer to see what the difference is and what the price should be.

What is traded in consent makes everybody content.

The mosque preaches honesty; the marketplace teaches fraud.

A fellow craftsman is your foe, even if he is your brother; a fellow craftsman is your brother, even if he is your foe.

Have one eye open when you sell, and both when you buy.

"Buyer beware."

Chapter 4

Company

Solitude is better than bad company.

Eat bitter, drink bitter, but don't live with the bitter one.

Show me your company, and I'll show you what you are.

"You can judge a person by the company they keep."

No road is too long with good company.

Good company is a feast.

Chapter 5

Education

Learn from the cradle to the grave.

(This proverb is attributed to the Prophet Mohammed.)

Repetition will teach the donkey.

"Practice makes perfect."

He whose father and mother did not educate, the days and the nights will educate.

"Experience is the best teacher."

Knowledge comes from school, character comes from home.

Learning is like healing: it comes step-by-step.

Science in each generation has its value and price. (Egypt)

Chapter 6

Family

The end of a bunch of grapes has sweet honey.

The youngest child is favored by his parents.

A thousand enemies without the house and not one within.

One enemy in the family can cause more harm than a thousand enemies outside the family.

Blood can never turn into water.

"Blood is thicker than water."

Your family may chew you, but they won't swallow you.

The house is our father's, and the strangers came to take over.

This proverb refers to forcing people off their property but can also be used to describe people who take over a party and don't leave room for the host's family.

The maternal uncle is a father.

Children are believed to take after their maternal uncles because mothers have primary responsibility for raising children and the children's mother and maternal uncles were raised in the same house. This proverb applies mostly to boys. Another version is "Two-thirds of a child takes after his maternal uncle."

Even the entrails of the bell quarrel together.

It is normal for families to have quarrels.

The cousin is the carrier of blood.

A tribe's reputation is its first line of defense. If its reputation or honor is weakened, they must be restored with revenge. The cousins from the father's side of the family are traditionally responsible for fighting for honor and taking revenge.

Build your son without building for him.

Hit your child and perfect his discipline.

Break a rib and two will grow.

The stick is from the heavens.

The three previous proverbs advise corporal punishment for children.

The soft-hearted never (properly) raise a child.

With children, there is worry; and without them, there is worry.

Children are like spots on a carpet: each one has a different shade.

Children send evil away.

Parents are too busy looking after the children to get into arguments.

A rose issued from thorns.

This proverb refers to a good child coming from bad parents.

Wear your size, mingle with your equal, and know the one who knows your father and grandfather.

If you are without loved ones, only dogs and cats will visit you. (Egypt)

Chapter 7

Fear

Frighten the beast before the beast frightens you.

Don't fear God, but fear the one who doesn't fear Him.

He who doesn't fear Moses's stick must fear Pharaoh's.

"Moses's stick" refers to God's law; "Pharaoh's stick" refers to the laws of the government.

He fears the shadow of his own ears.

"He is afraid of his own shadow."

If you fear, don't say; if you say, don't fear.

Fear sees in the dark.

Fear is the conscience of the weak.

Chapter 8

Food and Eating

His intestines are singing.

"His stomach is growling."

No shaking hands while eating.

If someone arrives at a house during a meal, they will just say the greeting, *"Assalamu alaikum"* (peace be upon you) and sit down and start eating. Shaking hands will be postponed until after the meal.

Talking at meals brings devils to the table.

Man's worst enemy is his belly.

The eye is the one that eats.

This proverb expresses the importance of the appearance of food and how it affects the taste of the food.

Excess food makes one ill; excess wealth corrupts.

To feed a satiated man is a waste.

This proverb refers to declining the offer of more food when dining at someone's home or to decline an invitation to dine when one is already full or not hungry.

Chapter 9
Friendship

No road is too steep that leads to a friend.

Have patience with your friend rather than lose him forever.

Play alone, and you will end up happy.

This proverb means you should be careful when choosing friends. It is also used to tell children to avoid certain other children and to warn businessmen to avoid bad traders.

An onion with (from) a friend is a roast lamb.

"It's the thought that counts."

Do not tell a friend anything you would conceal from an enemy.

The face you see every day you must not displease in any way.

There are bones of a thousand friends in a wolf's den.

Don't rinse the cup of friendship with vinegar.

A friend is a mirror of his friend.

"Your friends are a reflection of you."

Two things are at their best when old: wine and friends.

Oh God, deliver me from my friends. As for my enemies, I'll take care of them myself.

Chapter 10

God and Religion

Cast your line into the sea, and God will provide.

If God proposes the destruction of an ant, He allows wings to grow upon her.

Elevating a person beyond their capabilities can destroy them.

He who has no father has God.

Orphans, or anyone needing assistance, can depend on God to help them.

Fear the person who does not fear God.

God created life in six days.

"Rome was not built in a day."

No one saw God with their eyes!

This proverb advises one to use one's mind to reason.

There shall be no compulsion in religion.

(*The Holy Koran*, 2:256)*

Do good, cast thy bread upon the waters, and one day thou shalt be rewarded.

"Cast your bread upon the waters, for you will find it after many days." (Ecclesiastes 11:1)**

If you take a risk of faith and do a good deed or perform an act of charity, you will be rewarded. This proverb has also been interpreted to refer to the idea that a risky distribution of one's assets will yield great returns, or that one should make commitments that one cannot go back on.

---

* Passages from *The Holy Koran* are from 1956 translation by N.J. Dawood. Published by Penguin Classic.

** Passages from *The Holy Bible* are taken from the New King James Version. Copyright © 1982 by Thomas Nelson, Inc. Used by permission. All rights reserved.

May God make it easier for you.

The good Muslim will not hurt others by his hand or tongue.

(This proverb is attributed to the Prophet Mohammed.)

A good Muslim will leave what is not his.

(This proverb is attributed to the Prophet Mohammed.)

Chapter 11
Health

Cheerfulness is a sign of health.

The stomach is the home of illness.

(This proverb is attributed to the Prophet Mohammed.)

The medicine that heals all illness is time.

A doctor's hit is Fate's hit.

My health is better than my wealth, my ankles are better than my ankle rings, and my ears are better than my earrings. (Iraq)

To be in good health is a constant feast.

Health and extravagance won't stay together.

Each day that goes by and I am okay is a feast. (Egypt)

You'll always feel the wound that's inside your head. (Egypt)

Wash your face to feel better; clean your house to free your mind. (Egypt)

Chapter 12

Honesty

The righteous word hurts.

"The truth hurts."

The bullet that does not hit makes a noise.

Accusations that are not true are still painful.

I believe what you say; I am surprised at what you do.

"Actions speak louder than words."

He who has a wound in the head will touch it.

Someone who has committed a crime will draw attention and expose himself.

He has two faces and two tongues.

The snow will eventually melt, and we will be able to see the lawn.

The truth will come out eventually.

Follow the liar to the gate of the house.

To know if a liar is telling the truth, follow him around for a while, even to his house.

Long fingers.

"Sticky fingers."

This proverb refers to a thief.

Do you want the truth or its cousin?

He who praises himself is a liar.

Lying and stealing are next-door neighbors.

Pigeon flyer!

This saying is used to call someone a liar. A pigeon flyer is a person who keeps pigeons. They capture wild pigeons by releasing their flock when they see a wild pigeon flying by. The flock then guides the wild bird back to the cage, where it is held until it becomes a member of the flock. Pigeon flyers have a reputation of being dishonest because they sometimes capture other peoples' birds.

He who lies once will lie every time.

The distance to truth is four fingers.

Four fingers is the distance from your ears to your eyes.

Walk straight and make no mistakes to confuse your enemy.

Chapter 13

Leadership

The one who carries the standard must also know the way.

Their leader is their servant.

Many a chieftain ruins the land.

It is easier to lead a herd of a thousand camels than a company of two men.

They who can't obey can't command.

Treat your superior as a father, your equal as a brother, and your junior as a son.

If you want to be obeyed, command what is feasible.

Chapter 14

Love and Marriage

A loving heart won't see a fault.

The dough stuck. (Palestine)

This proverb describes a successful marriage. A Palestinian bride will stick a piece of dough above the groom's door before entering to symbolize that she will stick with the groom.

A hasty marriage is slow sorrow.

Choose your horse with your eyes and your spouse with your ears.

Listen to what others say about him or her before deciding to marry.

Look to the roots before you plant your trees.

Consider the family background before getting married.

If her household praises her, leave her; if her neighbors praise her, take her and run away with her.

When choosing a bride, you should listen to what others say about her.

There is a loaf for every wedding.

Every marriage has a chance.

Her wedding dress was sewn with his ax.

The groom had to toil before he could afford to get married.

The one who loves does not hate.

Hearts and streams: If they meet, they make rivers.

He is drowned in love up to his hair.

"He is head-over-heels in love."

The older the flame of love, the higher it rises.

The first wife is better even if she is a piece of mud. (Egypt)

Chapter 15

Luck

Luck comes like a turtle and goes like a gazelle.

When he started to trade in shrouds, people stopped dying.

Bad luck.

If your bad luck is asleep, don't wake it up.

Her sun shines at night.

Good luck.

Hey! Your beard is dipped in oil today.

It's your lucky day.

Your luck may get sick, but it doesn't die.

The unlucky and the hopeless have come together.

"Misery loves company."

Chapter 16

Neighbors

If your neighbor shaves, soak your beard in water.

It is good to have good relations with neighbors; so if your neighbor does something, such as shaving his beard, you should do the same.

If your neighbor dislikes you, change the gate of your house.

Good morning, neighbor. You mind your business, and I will mind mine.

"Good fences make good neighbors."

This proverb refers to both literal and figurative neighbors.

A bad neighbor sees only what enters, not what goes out.

A bad neighbor will only see your faults.

We didn't sell the house, we sold the neighbor.

Lean toward your nearby neighbor, rather than your faraway brother.

Chapter 17

The Past

Now that the pumpkin is large and round, it has forgotten about its past.

"The success has gone to his head."

This proverb describes a person who has forgotten where he came from.

Squeeze the past like a sponge, smell the present like a rose, and send a kiss to the future.

"Stop and smell the roses."

What is past is an image, what is to come is a wish. You have only this hour—take it.

You are the child of your past.
Time has changed.

"Those were the days."

Since the year of Noah.

"As old as the hills."

Chapter 18

Patience

Patience demolishes mountains.

"Patience is a virtue."

A seven-month child.

Someone who is always in a hurry.

Patience of Job.

This same proverb is used in the West.

Sitting on fire.

Waiting impatiently.

Why is your onion burnt?

This proverb is said to people in a rush.

Who is chasing you with a stick?

"What's the hurry?"

Haste brings forth failure.

"Haste makes waste."

Patience heals the broken bone.

Patience cures all hardships save folly.

The door of patience needs no doorman.

A Bedouin took revenge after forty years. It was said he was in a hurry.

Patience is a tree whose root is bitter but whose fruit is sweet.

There is no sweet time without going through hell. (Egypt)

Chapter 19

Politics and Government

The Pharaoh was asked what made him a tyrant. "No one stood in my way," he replied.

"All that is necessary for the triumph of evil is for good men to do nothing." (Edmund Burk [1729–1797] Irish political philosopher)

Politicians plan things no devil can think of. (Egypt)

If the monkey reigns, dance for it. (Egypt)

Wherever the turban turns, heads will turn with it. (Libya)

"The turban" refers to the ruler.

Politics has no religion. (Lebanon)

Chapter 20

Promises

An egg today is better than a chicken tomorrow.

You promised me earrings and I pierced my ears; You didn't deliver and I hurt my ears.

This proverb refers to a broken promise.

His day is a month, and his month is an age.

This proverb describes a person who does not keep promises.

People ought to stay as big as their words.

Slow down your promise, speed up your performance.

Chapter 21

Rhetoric

One ties up a donkey by its feet
and a person by his tongue.

He has a mouth that drips honey.

A smooth talker.

Keep your tongue inside (your mouth).

Keep your mouth shut.

Your speech and urine are alike.

"You have a gutter mouth."

Do not make it either long or short.

Get to the point.

When you have spoken the word, it reigns over you. When it is unspoken, you reign over it.

Apprentice your son to a barber, and he will learn to be a talker. (Iraq)

Barbers in Iraq are known to be talkative.

Argue in Persian, reproach in Turkish, and flatter in Arabic.

One word should do for two.

His words were like empty nutshells.

His words were hollow.

A man talks less as his intelligence grows.

What is in his heart is on the tip of his tongue.

Talking without thinking is like hunting without aiming. (Egypt)

Even if the speaker is crazy, the listener should be wise. (Egypt)

Chapter 22

Secrets

What remains a secret never was.

Give your counsel to a thousand, but your secret to no one.

Water once poured is never collected again.

You can't take back what you say.

Don't listen to a secret, and don't tell one.

Once a secret is told, it is no longer a secret.

Chapter 23

Silence

Silence is the wisdom of the few.

Silence is the most eloquent expression.

You can make amends more easily for your silence than for your speech.

When invited to talk, silence is a rebuke.

The fruit of silence is tranquility.

The tree of silence bears the fruit of peace.

Chapter 24

Sorrow

Laugh with people and weep alone.

Much sorrow teaches weeping.

This proverb is used to discourage someone from dwelling on sadness.

All things start small and grow big, except sorrow.

Chapter 25

Travel

Honor the traveler, even if he is an infidel.

(This proverb is attributed to the Prophet Mohammed.)

He who lives sees much; he who travels sees more.

Travel is both school and picnic.

He has been to Acre and Mecca.

This proverb describes someone who has been everywhere.

In every country, hammer a stake.

Make friends everywhere you go.

The old think of dying, the young think of wandering.

When God made Hell, he did not find it bad enough, so he made Mesopotamia—and added flies.

When God made the Sudan, he laughed.

To speak a peoples' tongue is safe conduct among them.

Chapter 26

Unity

A bundle of sticks is harder to break.

"There is strength in unity."

He who has a back (to protect him) will not be struck in his stomach.

It's good to have friends watching your back.

He is from the bones of the neck.

He is one of us.

A tree that does not shade its own base gets cut first. (Bedouin)

A family or clan that does not protect its members will not survive.

Chapter 27

War and Peace

Arms are present and reason is absent.

They who know war will not welcome it with a dance! (Iraq)

They who entered the land without making war could leave it in peace.

If land is conquered without war, the conqueror will give it up without war.

Only those who are afraid to be called cowards will go to war.

In peace they bury us old; in war we bury them young.

Pardon is the choicest flower of victory.

Peace with fear is no peace.

He has one foot at home and one in the stirrup. (Bedouin)

This proverb is used to describe a coward or someone who hesitates about going into battle.

In the ashes I see fire, and warfare ever starts with a spark.

We have created you from a male and a female, and made you into nations and tribes, that you might get to know one another. The noblest of you in God's sight is he who is most righteous. (The Holy Koran, 49:13)

This passage from the Koran encourages people to live in peace and be devout.

God does not love the aggressor. (The Holy Koran, 2:190)

If anyone attacks you, attack him as he attacked you. (The Holy Koran, 2:194)

"Life shall be for life, eye for eye, tooth for tooth, hand for hand, foot for foot." (Deuteronomy 19:21)

Chapter 28

Wealth and Poverty

On top of the wind.

This proverb is used to describe a wealthy person or someone with no worries.

He whose wealth perplexes him may buy pigeons and let them fly.

"A fool and his money are soon parted."

Rather a man without money than money without a man.

"At least you have your health."

He became a big shot.

"From rags to riches."

Let the loss be in wealth, not in dear ones.

Money can be compensated, but not friends or family.

Too much of a thing is like too little of it.

Lending is the scissors of friendship.

You are rich when not in need;
You are poor when you borrow a reed.

Leave the honey in the jar till the market is ajar.

"Save for a rainy day."

Bad money serves bad ends.

"Treasures of wickedness profit nothing." (Proverbs 10:2)

Money strays, and people bring it back home (by working).

Men gain money and money gains men.

If money is in your pocket, it is your servant; if not, you are its servant.

Health without fortune is an illness without pain.

The funeral of a rich person and a poor person's wedding are crowded.

Tears are the poor person's efforts.

To pretend you are rich will only make you poorer.

To empty a jar is not like filling it up.

Greed will lose what has been amassed.

No one is poor along the seashore. (Bedouin)

It's better to live near the sea than near a rich man. (Bedouin)

If water is present for ablution, the use of sand is discontinued.

When you are affluent, it is not necessary to have the same practices as the poor. (Islam prescribes ablution with sand when water is not available.)

Chapter 29

Wisdom

Wisdom surpasses power.

Wisdom is the tree of life.

Little wisdom tries the feet.

A wise person is like a rock: slow to warm and to cool.

A wise person's error is a thousand fold greater.

In every head, there is wisdom.

A wise person in their native town is like gold inside its mine.

A wise man’s day is worth a fool’s life.

Chapter 30

Women

The wise woman has much to say, but she keeps her silence.

The minister of the interior.

This proverb refers to the lady of the house.

Men are earners; women are builders (of homes).

A woman's advice is good for a woman.

Men don't like to admit women's wisdom, but they go back to them for counsel.

To him who spends his fortune to educate two daughters or sisters, Paradise will be due by the grace of God.

(*This proverb is attributed to the Prophet Mohammed.*)

A house with no woman is like a graveyard.

This proverb expresses the importance of the woman's role in domestic affairs.

The home was not built on ground but on the women.

Women are the counterparts of men.

(*This proverb is attributed to the Prophet Mohammed by Hadiths Abu Dawud and Tirmidhi.*)

Men and women are equal.

What no longer fits a woman will fit her daughter.

The best among you are those who are the best to their womenfolk.

(*This proverb is attributed to the Prophet Mohammed.*)

Chapter 31
Work

The devil tempts all men, but idle men tempt the devil.

"Idle hands are the devil's playground."

The basket with two handles can be carried by two.

"Many hands make work light."

God loves the person who perfects his work.

(*This proverb is attributed to the Prophet Mohammed.*)

He fasted and fasted, and then broke his fast with an onion.

This proverb applies when someone works hard but gets little reward.

There is blessing in getting up early in the morning.

"Early to bed, early to rise, makes a man healthy, wealthy, and wise."

The monkey has nothing to do but pluck hair.

This proverb describes unemployed or idle people.

Get it done, and then have fun.

"Work before play."

No sweet without sweat.

Either you like your vocation or you need it.

If you are good at it, it's a career; if not, it's noise.

If you want to go to the flour mill, you should not be bothered by the dust of the road.

"If you can't stand the heat, get out of the kitchen."

Test the carpenter at the knot.

Work in the sun; eat in the shade.

Night work ridicules the day.

Hands perish; their work doesn't.

Shorten your days, and your years will be longer.

Work for this world as though you will live forever, and prepare for the hereafter as though you will die tomorrow.

Chapter 32

Miscellaneous

If you want to cause him confusion,
give him a choice.

We sowed "if" and reaped "naught."

"If 'ifs' and 'buts' were candy and nuts, we'd all have a merry Christmas."

He licks the sky with his tongue, don't you know.

He is a wishful thinker.

Stay away . . . you will be sweeter.

"Absence makes the heart grow fonder."

Too many chefs burn the food.

"Too many cooks spoil the broth."

If you have no shame, do whatever you please.

People with no shame act selfishly.

Tether the horse near the donkey, and he will learn to "hee" or to "haw."

"He who lives with wolves will learn to howl."

Feed the mouth, and the eye will be bashful.

If you are generous to people, they will be ashamed if they are not generous to others.

The pan found its lid.

"Two peas in a pod."

This proverb applies when two people are seen together who are viewed as no good or who cannot benefit each other.

He who has a hand in the water is unlike one who has a hand in fire.

Attitudes are formed by circumstance.

Whoever is whipped is not like the one counting the strikes of the whip.

That which costs nothing gives plenty.

Do not abuse someone's generosity; if they give you something, do not take too much.

He whose house is made of glass must not throw stones at others.

"People who live in glass houses should not throw stones."

He who does not know you ignores you.

If you see people worshiping a calf, mow grass and feed it.

"When in Rome, do as the Romans do."

The envious will not prevail.

"Envy eats nothing but its own."

Sadness has come for joy; she found no place to take her.

This proverb is used when someone needs assistance that is not available.

The clever girl spins with the leg of a donkey.

This proverb means a good workman can work with any tools. It is used to criticize people who do poor work because they are lazy or blame their tools.

He who is bitten by a snake is afraid of dragging the rope.

"Once bitten, twice shy."

The absent has his excuse.

"The absent party is not so faulty."

Beating a dead person is a sin.

Do not attack someone who is defenseless.

He who does not see through the sieve is blind.

"He cannot see the forest for the trees."

Falsehood is failure.

Lies are always detected.

Close the door through which comes the draught, and be tranquil.

Also: *Close the door through which comes the wind.*

Eliminate sources of discomfort.

He whom you know is better than he whom you do not know.

"Better the devil you know than the devil you don't know."

If you owe a dog anything, call him "sir."

Another day, like that which is passing, will not come again.

"Make hay while the sun shines."

If you see a one-eyed man pass by, turn up a stone. (Palestine)

Some Palestinians use the term "one-eyed man" to refer to someone who is disagreeable. Some also believe seeing a one-eyed man is a bad omen. In either case, turning over a stone is believed to be a way to avoid undesirable consequences.

When you strike, hurt; when you feed a man, satiate him.

Don't go halfway.

The stars in heaven are nearer to you.

The outcome of something will not be good.

The water gives the lie to the diver.

"Put your money where your mouth is."

If someone pretends to be a diver, water will bring out the truth. This proverb can apply to anyone who is boasting.

Distract a dog with a bone.

Pay someone to stay silent about something.

The eye can see what the hand cannot reach.

Wanting something you cannot have.

Open confession is good for the soul.

Do a good deed and throw it in the sea.

Do not expect a reward for doing good.

Your good deeds will precede you.

The ignorant person is his own enemy.

Let them slap a thousand necks, but not mine.

Expression used to avoid trouble. (Slapping someone's neck is an insult.)

When the angels present themselves, the devils abscond.

A little wine gladdens the heart; a little more saddens the face.

Wine does not so much corrupt a man as much as greed does.

(This proverb is attributed to Caliph Omar, the second Caliph of Islam, seventh century AD.)

There is great harm in both (drinking and gambling), although they have some benefit for men; but their harm is far greater than their benefit. (*The Holy Koran*, 2:219)

Throw the needle, and it will click.

"You could hear a pin drop."

Hammer the iron while it is hot.

"Strike while the iron is hot."

Press the clay while it is soft, and plant the sapling while it is green.

"Strike while the iron is hot."

The third strike is fatal.

"The third time is a charm."

A good knight makes a good horse.

"A good husband makes a good wife."

If you treat someone well, they will treat you well.

Far from the eye, far from the heart.

"Out of sight, out of mind."

He drinks from a well, and he throws a stone into it.

"Do not bite the hand that feeds you."

Between the hammer and the anvil.

"Between a rock and a hard place."

He builds castles in the air.

"He has his head in the clouds."

The door of the house fits a camel.

"Don't let the door hit you on the way out."

You look at me with one eye; I will look at you with both eyes.
Also: *Serve me lunch, I'll serve you dinner.*

"You scratch my back, and I'll scratch yours." (This is also an Arab proverb.)

When a donkey climbs the minaret.

"When pigs fly."

Visit each other, and do not live close to one another.

It may be fire now, but tomorrow it will be ashes.

"This too shall pass."

Your fingers are not all the same.

People are different.

The world is small.

"It's a small world."

Go and ride the highest horse you have.

"Take your best shot."

Diamond cuts diamond.

"Fight fire with fire."

We are at the house of falsehood, and he is at the house of righteousness.

"Don't speak ill of the dead."

The flute player dies, but his fingers are still moving.

"Old habits die hard."

He sees blindness and acts blind.

"He turns a blind eye."

He floats on an inch of water.

This proverb describes a person who is full of himself.

He whitewashed his face.

To make someone proud. If someone makes someone proud, they might say he "made his face white." The opposite would be "He blackened his face."

The mountains of kohl (eye shadow) will be exhausted by the kohl sticks.

"Nothing lasts forever."

Kohl was first used by the ancient Egyptians and later adopted by the Arabs to protect their eyes from the sun. Both Arab men and women used kohl. The custom was later picked up by Western women for purely cosmetic purposes.

I have baked and kneaded him.

"I know him like the back of my hand."

Jingle your coins, and people will gather.

This is said to lonely people.

A dog's tail is never straight.

"Even though you put a dog's tail in a mould, it will always come out curled."

This is used to describe someone who will not change their bad habits.

Humiliated you are, oh you borrower!

"Neither a borrower nor a lender be." (William Shakespeare, *Hamlet*)

Associate with those who are happy, and you become happy.

"Keep good company, and you shall be one of them."

A little bit of good is better than none.

"Something is better than nothing."

He added water to mud.

"He added insult to injury."

It has taken awhile for the moon to appear.

"Long time no see."

A storm in a cup.

This proverb is said when a big fight starts over a small matter.

A sip of water.

"A piece of cake."

The soap of Arabs is their beards.

This proverb is used to describe men who do not wash after eating. It is said that traditional Bedouins prefer not to use soap but instead wipe their hands on their beards after eating. Also, when someone does a bad deed, a Bedouin might say, "Wipe it in my beard."

He started swallowing his saliva.

This proverb refers to eating one's words.

Pure! Oh yogurt!

This proverb is used when former enemies reconcile.

Safe and sound.

The same proverb is used in the West.

They hit him with the evil eye.

Some Arabs, especially older women, believe that if you look at someone or something with "the evil eye" of jealousy or envy, you will bring them bad luck. They might say this when a child is sick and they believe it is because someone looked at the child and was envious of the parents. Also, if something happens to your car or some other nice object, this proverb applies, to say that it was because someone looked at it and was jealous.

My bird flew away, and someone else took it.

This proverb is used when someone causes you to lose an opportunity. It can also be said when your significant other leaves you for someone else.

Beat the drum, and I will blow the pipe.

"One hand washes the other."

He left the festival without dried peas.
(Egypt and Palestine)

This proverb is used whenever someone returns from someplace empty-handed. Dried peas are a traditional snack for people to bring home from festivals (*muulid*) in Egypt and Palestine.

Like beating a drum near a deaf person.

"Like talking to a brick wall."

Sleep flew out of my eyes.

This proverb applies when a person cannot sleep.

His mind flew away.

He has lost his mind.

What the eye does not see, the heart does not grieve over.

In dire circumstances, there is neither a brother nor a friend.

"Every man for himself."

A blind woman shaves an insane one.

"The blind leading the blind."

This proverb is used to describe an impossible situation or when a person is trying to do a job he can't handle.

He got what he wanted in the cold.

"Easy as pie."

"In the cold" means the person got something with little effort or resistance.

Your wedding came first.

This proverb expresses the importance of keeping commitments. It is also said when there is a funeral on a day that a wedding was planned. The family planning the wedding goes to the family having the funeral to offer condolences and ask permission to still have the wedding. This proverb would then be used to give permission for the wedding.

It's like Satan hoping to enter Paradise.

This proverb refers to hoping for the impossible.

My mind is not a notebook.

This is used when someone forgets something.

Hello, our door!

"It's good to be home!"

On the wheel's rim.

This proverb is used to describe a poor person.

We live and we see.

"I cannot believe my eyes."

Close one eye and open the other one.

"In the blink of an eye."

Like a villager visiting the city.

"Like a fish out of water."

There are good men, and there are fake men.

Call a one-eyed person one-eyed.

"Call a spade a spade."

I have goose flesh.

"I have goose bumps."

He has a white heart.

"He has a heart of gold."

White is associated with purity. The opposite is black, so someone with bad intentions would be said to have a black heart.

Much laughter dispels gravity.

If you laugh too much, you can lose people's respect.

Every person sleeps on the side that gives him most comfort.

"To each his own."

(Cicero [106 BC - 43 BC] Roman author, orator, and politician)

Every knot has an unraveler.

Everything forbidden is desired.

"Forbidden fruit is the sweetest."

Every rise has a fall.

"Every tide has its ebb."

His word is one word.

"His word is his bond."

Too much pulling will cause looseness.

This proverb encourages people to not be too extreme in solving problems, lest they cause a new problem.

The dog of the sheikh is a sheikh.

Each one has his own troubles.

"Every path has a puddle."

We are all children of nine months.

Everyone is created equal.

In prison and in death, all people are equal.

The camels of the sultan are also unshod.

Everyone is equal.

Men are born equal like the teeth of a comb.

(*This proverb is attributed to the Prophet Mohammed.*)

Eat olive oil and bump your head against the wall. (Palestine)

Olive oil is so healthful that if you eat it, you can hit your head against a wall and not get hurt.

For the rose, the thorn is watered.

This refers to the act of helping someone because of family or business relations, even though the person does not deserve it.

Refrain from telling me that this was and that was not.

Don't make excuses.

He failed to bring the mulberry of the Levant or the grapes of Yemen.

This proverb is used to describe someone who returns from an endeavor without accomplishing anything, or someone who does not finish a task.

No one saw, no one knew.

This proverb refers to doing something secretly.

He wore the hiding cap.

This proverb applies when someone has not been seen for a long time.

An American plaster.

This proverb is used to describe a person who visits and does not leave. (American plaster is known for its good quality and ability to stick to walls.)

The mouse started playing in my breast pocket.

"I smell a rat."

If the world gets emptied of good people, it will perish.

To chatter and to knead (a question).

"To beat a dead horse."

Nothing new under the sun.

He who stays with people for forty days becomes one of their number.

From knocking till good-bye.

This proverb means "the whole time."

Don't play with him.

"Don't mess with him."

He rented the upper floor (his brain).

This proverb is said when someone acts stupid.

His upper floor is rented.

He is crazy.

No stranger except Satan.

This proverb is used to tell someone they are always welcome.

Four things do not come back: the spoken word, the sped arrow, the past life, and the neglected opportunity.

His gallbladder is out.

This proverb is used when someone is sad or stubborn.

He is not within himself.

"He is not himself."

Who squeezed your tail?

"Mind your own business."

I went far away.

"I was way off."

Half and half.

"So-so."

He saved his feathers.

"He saved his own skin."

He shook his hand away from someone.

To break with someone.

He slept in the house of his aunt.

To spend the night in jail or prison.

Falling between two fires.

"Between a rock and a hard place."

Show us the width of your shoulders.

"Go away."

God creates forty people of a kind.

This proverb is said when you see someone that looks like someone else.

A honey day and an onion day.

"Some days are diamonds, some days are stones."

A little hole can sink a big ship.

One stone can disturb a flock of birds.

A pebble can support a big jar, but a big jar cannot bear a pebble (when thrown at it).

Eat me like a lion, but don't bite me like a dog.

If your sword is broken, make a sickle out of it.

If you set your house on fire, you will warm up with it once.

Barking dogs don't bite.

An ant eats more than its head can take.

People can perform jobs bigger than themselves.

A dog doesn't bite its tail.

"Don't bite the hand that feeds you."

Even a goat has a beard.

"Don't judge a book by its cover."

A beard is sign of respectability.

Don't let turbans deceive you!

This proverb means that looks can be deceiving. (Turbans are worn by the clergy but can also be worn by laypeople.)

Not all round things are walnuts, nor all long things bananas.

"All that glitters is not gold."

Applause is the virtue of the applauder rather than the applauded.

He who asks darkens half of his face; he who rejects him who asks darkens his entire face.

Be civil in public and gentle in private.

Don't do in private what you don't do in public.

Her bread is baked, and her water is in the jar.

This proverb refers to being carefree.

One cannot eat a nut before breaking it.

"You can't make an omelet without breaking some eggs."

Charity banishes evil.

Have mercy on those below you, so that the one above you may have mercy on you.

Complain in vain, and you'll cause pain.

If the mountain doesn't come to you, go to the mountain.

"If the mountain won't come to Mohammed, then Mohammed must go to the mountain."

This refers to taking matters into your own hands to get something done, instead of waiting passively for the thing to accomplish itself. According to legend, the Prophet Mohammed was once asked to prove he was a prophet by performing a miracle, so he ordered a mountain to come to him. When it did not move, Mohammed said this was proof of God's mercy because if it moved, they would have all been crushed by it. He then went to the mountain to thank God for his mercy. However, the story is not in the Koran or *Hadith*, and most Muslims say the Prophet never attempted to perform miracles. The story and the Western version (above in quotes) of the original Arab proverb first appeared in an essay by Francis Bacon in the seventeenth century and is probably a Western invention based on the Bible passage about faith moving mountains.

Take advice from the one who arrived a night before you.

Give counsel to your friend; let it be sweet or bitter.

Give counsel to a fool and gain a foe.

No right judgment without counsel.

Fish begin to stink at the head.

The market of debauchery is always open.

There is but one way to enter life, but the exit gates are without number.

Praise a day in the evening and a person at the end of their line.

Deeds are to be judged by intentions.

"It's the thought that counts."

Request from a stranger, ask from a friend, and demand from a rival.

The path of destiny has many crossroads.

She fled from the leak and came under the spout.

"Out of the frying pan and into the fire."

This proverb refers to going from a bad situation to one that is worse.

He whose place is not orderly and neat, his barley will eat up his wheat.

Envy is a bone: If it sticks in your throat, it will kill you.

A tongue of praise is an eye of envy.

A fool's error is a red herring; a wise person's slip is a big fish.

We commit errors because we are hasty; we learn from them because we are wise.

He sees a dome in a grain and a camel in a bug.

"Making a mountain out of a molehill."

A person's face is an open book, if one can read it.

Real faults appear only when a thing is finished.

Favors are treasures: Take care with whom you deposit them.

Don't ask for a favor if you don't need it.

Don't praise the beginning
before you see the end.

Admire with your heart and flatter with your tongue.

You're a loser if you argue with a fool.

When force is the master, reason’s house is the first to be demolished.

They who forgive, God will forgive them.

“I forgive but . . .” is not forgiveness.

Forgive your enemy and make them weaker.

God loves the charitable.
(*The Holy Koran*, 2:195)

"We make a living by what we get; we make a life by what we give." (Sir Winston Churchill)

If you search for God, you will find Him.

"Seek and you will find." (Mathew 7:7)

If God shuts one door, He will open another.

Throw good behind you, and you will find it ahead of you.

Big nose, great character.

He who can steal a minaret can hide it too.

If you are at home, take your time.

In every home, there is a sewer.

The first guest is the host of the second. (Iraq)

A guest is the owner of the house for three days.

A house full of people is better than a house full of gold.

Imitation is blind praise.

"Imitation is the sincerest form of flattery."

It is better to know than not to know.

Your sun is high!

You are late!

Slower than Noah's crow.

Noah sent crows to look for land when the rains stopped, but they never returned.

The wise person pauses; the mad person crosses the river.

"Look before you leap."

Don't laud a gown before you have it on, nor a man before you prove him.

Every man is a boy in his own home.

If your mind is not with you, you won't find it anywhere you go.

Her tongue is dates, but her hands are wood.

This proverb is said of a miser.

A thousand times "Miser!" rather than once "Needy!"

A good name will not die; a bad name is already dead.

Opportunities pass quickly and return slowly.

If your wind blows, winnow your threshing floor.

Don't utter "broad beans" before they are in your storeroom.

"Don't count your chickens before they are hatched."

Those who plant thorns won't get grapes.

"Whatever a man sows, that he will also reap."
(Galatians 6:7)

People are locks; for each there is a unique key.

People are more like their times than their parents.

Steady drops pierce rocks.

Unwrapping the presents is wrapping up the friendship.

It is customary to not open presents in the presence of the giver.

Don't dig deep, least a viper comes out for you.

Don't provoke people.

Don't push your boat away after crossing a river.

"Don't burn your bridges."

Beware of still water and of the silent one.

"Still waters run deep."

It's a "butchers' quarrel." (Iraq)

In Iraqi meat markets, if there is a quarrel, knives are put away first.

He who gives a slap will receive its brother.

The weeds are watered, thanks to the rose bushes.

Rumors last seven days; news takes its time.

Don't stir what is laying still; don't stop what is moving.

"Let sleeping dogs lie."

Run away while your eyes are dry.
Before you're trapped and made to cry.

Summer's mat is large.

"Summertime, and the livin' is easy."

(From the song "Summertime" composed by George Gershwin for the 1935 opera *Porgy and Bess*)

In the summer, you can move around and sit anywhere.

The eyes are the spoon of speech.

The eyes can "measure" what is said.

Everyone is to drink from their own roof.

Everyone has to be self-reliant. (Drinking from your own roof refers to the well that is filled with rainwater from the roof.)

The bell calls people to church, but it stays outside. (Lebanon)

Servants stay out of sight when not needed.

A shared pot never boils.

Don't wear two shirts while your uncle goes naked.

Sharing carries blessing.

Don't start a job you don't intend to finish.

We've not yet spun or woven.

We are just getting started.

Two-thirds of the way lie before the threshold.

If your stone is too big, you can't throw it.

"Don't bite off more than you can chew."

A stone on the road.

This proverb describes a useless thing.

Draw on water and pinch a stone.

This proverb refers to doing something that is futile.

Someone's cake is being baked on someone else's burning beard.

Under the robe, there is something peculiar!

Something is suspicious.

Sweets, sweets, I like sweets: Fill my mouth with sweets, or else I'll leave it open.

This is a threat of blackmail.

Stay a wheel if hard times roll over you.

"Roll with the punches."

Barking dogs won't bother the moon.

"Barking at the moon."

His beard is plucked out.

He is in big trouble.

One arrow is for you, another is against you.

This proverb refers to life's ups and downs.

The veil covers shortcomings; exposure uncovers pockets. (Egypt)

Not wearing a veil is more expensive because you have to maintain more clothes and keep up with fashion.

Big fish eat up small fish, and the weak are doomed to perish.

Beware of the weapon of the weak!

The weapon of the weak is their prayers against those who wrong them.

A kind welcome is better than a tasty dinner.

You are welcome as many times as the steps that took you from there up to here. (Iraq)

Let me go lest I cry; hold me tight lest I fall!

This proverb means to be willy-nilly.

At times, you look for witnesses; at times, witnesses look for you.

Stool witness. (Iraq)

In Iraq, a “stool witness” is a professional witness who sits in front of a public building and offers to sign routine documents as a witness.

The world is a mirror: It looks at you the same way you look at it.

The world shows you the horse and gives you the donkey.

Worries were asked how they entered.
"Through the open door," they answered.

Had mountains men's worries, they would have collapsed.

Take care not to let cares take you.

What a wonder is the pen: It drinks darkness and utters light.

❧

No after Yes is but a decline, Yes after No is just fine.

❧

If life gets tight, loosen it by migration. (Bedouin)

Moving is a way to escape the problems of the desert and of life.

Every horse in the wild is a runner. (Bedouin)

This proverb is used to mock someone who is boasting. In the wild, there would be no witnesses to their exaggeration.

Just as one who's with calf will give birth, so he who sows will reap. (Bedouin)

His feedbag is fixed on his neck. (Bedouin)

He is self-reliant.

He who is making coffee has no back.
(Bedouin)

A guest should not be offended if the host turns his back on them while he is preparing coffee and providing for his guest.

Since I am drowning, why should I fear getting wet?

Things couldn't get any worse.

Keep your dog hungry, and it will follow you.

"Never give a customer all he wants."

If you need something badly, from even a dog, call him "Sir."

Give him your finger,
he will demand your arm.

"Give him an inch, he'd take a mile."

He who acts like a sheep will be eaten by wolves.

Do not open a door you cannot close.

An empty rifle will frighten two men.

The man at whom an unloaded rifle is pointed and the man pointing it, who knows his threat is empty, will both be frightened.

If you cannot bite, do not show your teeth.

I asked, "Why are you so polite?" He replied, "It is the art of God."

An Egyptian morning. (Egypt)

This saying is used in Egypt by Egyptians and expats alike when they are having a challenging morning.

She/he is the daughter/son of a shoe.

This proverb serves as a nasty insult.

If a flower dies, it will keep its good smell. (Egypt)

Your good deeds will remain after you are gone.

Walk with glory, not with a big belly. (Egypt)

Some people eat a date, and others throw its stones. (Egypt)

If you do not take the whole peach, you'll end up with only its juice. (Egypt)

Lebanese write books, Egyptians publish them, and Iraqis read them.

A boiling pot with a lid that's too tight will blow up the kitchen.

At the beginning of the protests in Egypt in 2011, an Egyptian army general was asked about the army strategy for dealing with the protesters and he responded with this proverb. It is similar to the Western saying "blow off steam," which originates from the act of relieving pressure in steam boilers to prevent damage.

Also by Stephen J. McGrane

Sit Crooked and Speak Straight:
Doing Business on the Arabian Peninsula.

Llumina Press, ISBN: 978-1-60594-031-1,
Paperback, 168 pages, 2008.
http://sitcrookedandspeakstraight.com/

'Trust in God but Tie Your Camel'
and Other Arab Proverbs.

Llumina Press, ISBN: 978-1-60594-359-6,
Paperback, 161 Pages, 2009.

Both books are available from Llumina.com,
Amazon.com, and Barnsandnoble.com.

www.ingramcontent.com/pod-product-compliance
Lightning Source LLC
Chambersburg PA
CBHW030010290326
41934CB00005B/292
* 9 7 8 1 6 2 5 5 0 4 5 3 1 *